Table of Contents

Meet the...

How to Use This Book

The ability to recognize word family patterns is an important part of learning to read. The stories and activities in this book help students increase their reading vocabulary while practicing the essential phonological skills of onset and rime. Each unit follows a consistent format:

Introduce the Word Family

Model blending each initial sound with the word family phoneme. Ask students to point to each picture as they repeat the word after you. Then have students write the word family phoneme on the lines. Next, students practice reading and writing sight words from the story by completing the Story Words to Know activity at the bottom of the page.

Read the Story

Instruct students to follow along as you read the story aloud. Then have students underline each word family word in the story or poem. Have students read the story again using one of the following methods:

- Read silently
- Echo read
- Choral read

Complete the Activity Pages

The activity pages after each story practice the word family presented and follow a consistent format, leading students to work independently.

Use the Slider

The slider is a quick and easy tool that encourages repeated practice of word family vocabulary, leading to increased oral reading fluency.

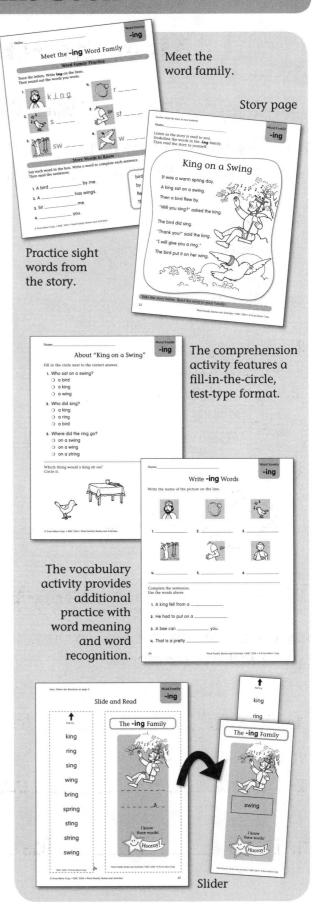

Meet the word family.

Story page

Practice sight words from the story.

The comprehension activity features a fill-in-the-circle, test-type format.

The vocabulary activity provides additional practice with word meaning and word recognition.

Slider

Name_____

Meet the **-ack** Word Family

Word Family Practice

Trace the letters. Write **ack** on the lines.
Then sound out the words you wrote.

1.  b a c k

2.  tr ___ ___ ___

3.  sn ___ ___ ___

4.  qu ___ ___ ___

5.  st ___ ___ ___

6.  bl ___ ___ ___

Story Words to Know

Say each word in the box. Write a word to complete each sentence.
Then read the sentences.

1. Do you _____ to eat candy?

2. I like to _____ candy.

3. I can _____ fast.

eat
run
like

Name _____

Listen as the story is read to you.
Underline the words in the **-ack** family.
Then read the story to yourself.

I Like

I like to wear my black hat.

I like to eat a hot dog for a snack.

I like to lie on my back.

I like to run on the track.

I like to put cards in a stack.

quack

I like to hear the ducks say, "Quack!"

Take the story home. Read the story to your family.

Word Family Stories and Activities • EMC 3354 • © Evan-Moor Corp.

About "I Like"

Fill in the circle next to the correct answer.

1. The boy likes to wear his black _____.
   - ○ hat
   - ○ rack
   - ○ sack

2. The boy likes to lie on his _____.
   - ○ sack
   - ○ back
   - ○ rack

3. The boy likes to hear the ducks say, "_____."
   - ○ Snack
   - ○ Sack
   - ○ Quack

Circle the pictures that show things that belong in your backp**ack**.

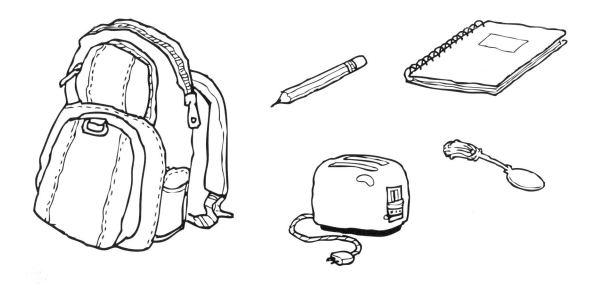

Name _____

Write **-ack** Words

Write the name of the picture on the line.

1. _____   2. _____   3. _____

4. _____   5. _____   6. _____

Complete the sentences.
Use the words above.

1. Jack ate a _____.

2. The snack was in a _____.

3. You can put a lot on a _____.

4. The bowl had a big _____ in it.

Word Family Stories and Activities • EMC 3354 • © Evan-Moor Corp.

Note: Cut out the slider parts along the dashed lines.
Then slip the word strip through the slider window.

Slide and Read

↑

Pull Up

back

lack

pack

rack

black

crack

quack

shack

snack

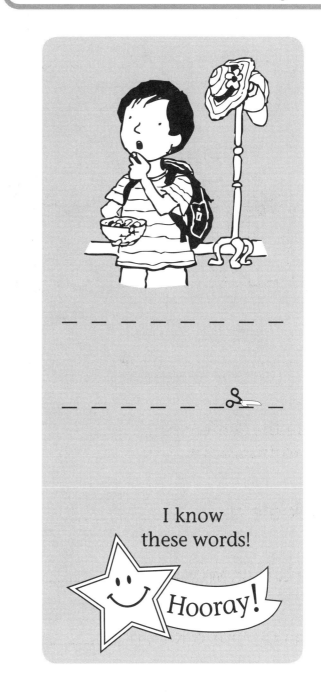

The **-ack** Family

I know
these words!

Hooray!

crack

pack

back

shack

snack

rack

end of
-ack family

quack

black

crack

quack

shack

snack

back

pack

Name _____

Meet the **-and** Word Family

Word Family Practice

Trace the letters. Write **and** on the lines.
Then sound out the words you wrote.

1.  b a n d

2.  s _ _ _

3.  st _ _ _

4. 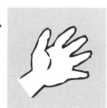 h _ _ _

5.  l _ _ _

6.  comm _ _ _

Story Words to Know

Say each word in the box. Write a word to complete each sentence.
Then read the sentences.

1. Will you _____ with me?

2. _____ to the music.

3. Can you _____ me that toy?

give

play

Listen

Name _____

Listen as the story is read to you.
Underline the words in the **-and** family.
Then read the story to yourself.

It Is Grand

It is grand
to listen to the band.

It is grand
to play in the sand.

It is grand
to stand on your hand.

It is grand
to give a command.

It is grand!

Take the story home. Read the story to your family.

10   Word Family Stories and Activities • EMC 3354 • © Evan-Moor Corp.

Name _____

About "It Is Grand"

Fill in the circle next to the correct answer.

1. It is grand to listen _____.
   ○ in the sand
   ○ to the band
   ○ on your hand

2. It is grand to play _____.
   ○ in the sand
   ○ to the band
   ○ a command

3. It is grand to stand on your _____.
   ○ sand
   ○ band
   ○ hand

Yes or no?
Circle the answer.

1. Have you ever played in the sand?

 yes   no

2. Can you stand on your hand?

 yes   no

Name_____

Write **-and** Words

Complete the sentences.
Use the words.

> hand   sand   land   stand

1. I can play in the _____.

2. My _____ hurts.

3. Dogs live on _____.

4. The baby can _____.

Find the word that matches the picture.
Circle it.

1.    grand   land

2.   sand   band

3.   stand   hand

Slide and Read

Pull Up

band

hand

land

sand

brand

gland

grand

stand

command

The -and Family

I know
these words!

Hooray!

Word Family Stories and Activities • EMC 3354 • © Evan-Moor Corp.

band

hand

sand

land

brand

brand

end of
-and family

band

gland

hand

stand

sand

command

brand

grand

gland

Name_____

Meet the -**atch** Word Family

Word Family Practice

Trace the letters. Write **atch** on the lines.
Then sound out the words you wrote.

1.  c a t c h

2.  m _ _ _ _

3. 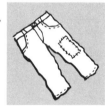 p _ _ _ _

4.  h _ _ _ _

5.  l _ _ _ _

6. 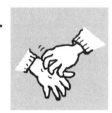 scr _ _ _ _

Story Words to Know

Say each word in the box. Write a word to complete each sentence.
Then read the sentences.

1. It is _____ to stand on one foot.

2. The hen lives in a big _____.

3. My dog _____ for me at the bus stop.

henhouse

waits

hard

Name _____

Listen as the story is read to you.
Underline the words in the **-atch** family.
Then read the story to yourself.

Scratch

I have a hen.

I call her Scratch.

Scratch can run fast.

She is hard to catch!

Scratch runs into her henhouse.

And I close the latch.

She sits on her eggs and waits for them to hatch.

Crack, crack, crack!

1, 2, 3, chicks that match!

You are a mama now, Scratch!

Take the story home. Read the story to your family.

16   Word Family Stories and Activities • EMC 3354 • © Evan-Moor Corp.

Name_____

About "Scratch"

Fill in the circle next to the correct answer.

1. Scratch is _____.
  ○ a dog
  ○ a cat
  ○ a hen

2. Scratch can _____.
  ○ run fast
  ○ jump
  ○ sleep

3. What did the eggs do?
  ○ latch
  ○ hatch
  ○ scratch

Draw a line to make a match.

1.  •   • latch

2.  •   • Scratch

3.  •   • hatch

Name _____

Write **-atch** Words

Complete the sentences.
Use the words.

patch   catch   match   batch

1. I want to _____ a fish.

2. My pants have a _____.

3. My socks do not _____.

4. Mom made a _____ of cookies.

Look at each picture.
Write a sentence about it.

1.    _____
   _____.

2.    _____
   _____.

Note: Cut out the slider parts along the dashed lines.
Then slip the word strip through the slider window.

Slide and Read

↑

Pull Up

batch

catch

hatch

latch

match

patch

scratch

thatch

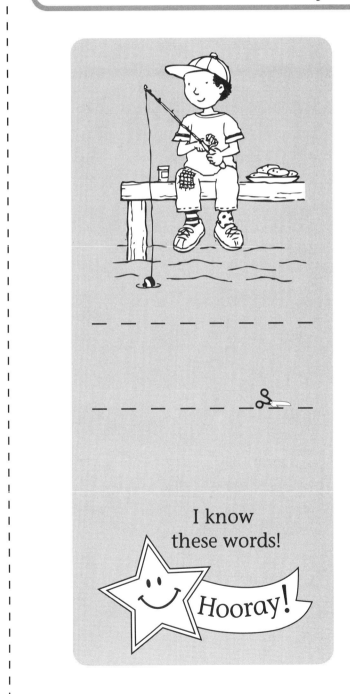

The **-atch** Family

I know
these words!

Hooray!

batch

catch

hatch

latch

patch

match

end of
-atch family

batch

scratch

hatch

match

catch

latch

thatch

patch

scratch

Meet the **-ell** Word Family

Word Family Practice

Trace the letters. Write **ell** on the lines.
Then sound out the words you wrote.

1.  b e l l

2. 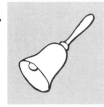 y _ _ _

3.  sm _ _ _

4.  w _ _ _

5.  sh _ _ _

6.  sp _ _ _

Story Words to Know

Say each word in the box. Write a word to complete each sentence.
Then read the sentences.

1. What do you _____?

2. _____ the bell.

3. I want _____ to eat.

4. I have not _____ that before.

> Ring
>
> something
>
> need
>
> done

Name _____

Listen as the story is read to you.
Underline the words in the **-ell** family.
Then read the story to yourself.

Just Tell Nell!

Do you need something done?

Just tell Nell!

Tell Nell to ring the bell.

Tell Nell to find a shell.

Tell Nell to smell.

Tell Nell to yell.

Tell Nell to spell.

Do you need something done?

Just tell Nell!

DOG
D...O...G!

Name_____

About "Just Tell Nell!"

Fill in the circle next to the correct answer.

1. Tell Nell to ring _____.
   - ○ the bell
   - ○ the smell
   - ○ the yell

2. Tell Nell to find _____.
   - ○ a bell
   - ○ a shell
   - ○ a well

3. Do you need something done?
   - ○ Just yell!
   - ○ Just smell!
   - ○ Just tell Nell!

Which things smell good?
Circle the pictures.

Name _____

Write **-ell** Words

Write the name of the picture on the line.

1. _____

2. _____

3. _____

4. _____

5. _____

6. _____

Complete the sentences.
Use the words above.

1. Please do not _____.

2. A turtle has a _____.

3. Make a wish at the _____.

4. Ring the _____!

Word Family Stories and Activities • EMC 3354 • © Evan-Moor Corp.

Note: Cut out the slider parts along the dashed lines.
Then slip the word strip through the slider window.

Slide and Read

↑

Pull Up

bell

fell

Nell

sell

tell

well

yell

shell

smell

spell

The **-ell** Family

_ _ _ _ _ _ _

_ _ _ _ _ _ ✂ _

I know
these words!

Hooray!

Word Family Stories and Activities • EMC 3354 • © Evan-Moor Corp.

fell

bell

Nell

sell

tell

yell

end of
-ell family

well

shell

smell

sell

spell

yell

tell

bell

smell

Meet the **-ent** Word Family

Word Family Practice

Trace the letters. Write **ent** on the lines.
Then sound out the words you wrote.

1.  b e n t

2.  d _ _ _

3.  K _ _ _ _

4.  c _ _ _ _

5.  t _ _ _

6.  Br _ _ _ _

Story Words to Know

Say each word in the box. Write a word to complete each sentence.
Then read the sentences.

1. I have two _____ and one cent.

2. I _____ my bike.

3. Put the apples _____ the bag.

4. My _____ has a dent.

> bike
>
> rode
>
> into
>
> dollars

Name _____

Listen as the story is read to you.
Underline the words in the **-ent** family.
Then read the story to yourself.

The Bike

Kent had a bike.

It was old and bent.

He lent the bike to Brent.

Brent rode the bike into a tent.

Then the bike had a dent!

Brent went to a shop to fix the dent.

He spent five dollars and one cent.

Brent gave the bike back to Kent.

Now the bike did not have a dent.

But it was still old and bent.

Take the story home. Read the story to your family.

28   Word Family Stories and Activities • EMC 3354 • © Evan-Moor Corp.

Name_____

About "The Bike"

Fill in the circle next to the correct answer.

1. First?
   - ○ Trent hit a tent.
   - ○ Brent spent a cent.
   - ○ Kent lent a bike to Brent.

2. Next?
   - ○ Brent fixed a dent.
   - ○ Brent spent a cent.
   - ○ Brent hit a tent.

3. Last?
   - ○ Trent hit a tent.
   - ○ Brent gave the bike back to Kent.
   - ○ Brent spent a cent.

Draw a line to make a match.

1.  •

2.  •

3.  •

• Brent hit a tent.

• Brent spent five dollars and one cent.

• The bike was bent.

Name _____

Write **-ent** Words

Write the name of the picture on the line.

1. _____   2. _____   3. _____

4. _____   5. _____   6. _____

Use the words above to write your own sentences.

1. _____.

2. _____.

3. _____.

4. _____.

5. _____.

6. _____.

Note: Cut out the slider parts along the dashed lines.
Then slip the word strip through the slider window.

Slide and Read

↑
Pull Up

bent

cent

dent

lent

rent

sent

tent

went

spent

The **-ent** Family

I know
these words!

Hooray!

cent

dent

bent

lent

rent

end of
-ent family

went

sent

spent

lent

dent

cent

bent

spent

rent

went

Meet the **-est** Word Family

Word Family Practice

Trace the letters. Write **est** on the lines.
Then sound out the words you wrote.

1.  b e s t

2.  r _ _ _

3.  w _ _ _

4.  n _ _ _

5.  t _ _ _

6.  cr _ _ _

Story Words to Know

Say each word in the box. Write a word to complete each sentence.
Then read the sentences.

1. I must _____ a test.

2. A bird can _____.

3. Try _____.

4. _____ I tried to fly.

again

fly

Once

take

Name _____

Listen as the story is read to you.
Underline the words in the **-est** family.
Then read the story to yourself.

Fly West

Little bird, up in a nest,

Little bird, with a funny crest,

Do not sit and take a rest,

You must fly west.

Try it once, and do your best,

Try again, just take the test!

Fly and fly and do not rest,

You can fly west from your nest!

Word Family Stories and Activities • EMC 3354 • © Evan-Moor Corp.

About "Fly West"

Fill in the circle next to the correct answer.

1. What is in the nest?
   - ○ a test
   - ○ a bird
   - ○ a bat

2. What is the test?
   - ○ to try to fly
   - ○ to rest
   - ○ to make a nest

3. Where is the bird going to fly?
   - ○ east
   - ○ west

Circle two things that birds can do.

ride a bike

eat a pest

fly west

Name_____

Write **-est** Words

Write the name of the picture on the line.

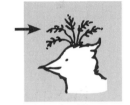

1. _____

2. _____

3. _____

4. _____

5. _____

6. _____

Complete the sentences. Use the words above.

1. The bird is in a _____.

2. The bird has a _____.

3. The bird will fly _____.

4. I did well on the _____.

5. The man has a _____.

6. You must _____.

Word Family Stories and Activities • EMC 3354 • © Evan-Moor Corp.

Note: Cut out the slider parts along the dashed lines.
Then slip the word strip through the slider window.

Slide and Read

↑

Pull Up

best

nest

pest

rest

test

vest

west

chest

crest

The -est Family

I know
these words!

Hooray!

best

rest

nest

pest

test

chest

end of
-est family

vest

west

crest

chest

test

pest

best

nest

vest

Word Family Stories and Activities • EMC 3354 • © Evan-Moor Corp.

Name_____

Meet the **-ick** Word Family

Word Family Practice

Trace the letters. Write **ick** on the lines.
Then sound out the words you wrote.

1.  s i c k

2.  k _ _ _

3. 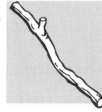 st _ _ _

4.  ch _ _ _

5.  l _ _ _

6. 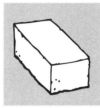 br _ _ _

Story Words to Know

Say each word in the box. Write a word to complete each sentence.
Then read the sentences.

1. He does not like _____ sick.

2. He _____ to get out of bed.

3. He feels _____ now.

better

being

wanted

Name _____

Listen as the story is read to you.
Underline the words in the **-ick** family.
Then read the story to yourself.

Nick's Chick

Nick was sick.

It was not fun to feel sick.

He wanted to get better quick.

Mom gave Nick a toy chick.

The toy chick did a trick.

It went "click, click, click."

It ran up a stick.

The chick made Nick forget about being sick.

Take the story home. Read the story to your family.

40

Word Family Stories and Activities • EMC 3354 • © Evan-Moor Corp

About "Nick's Chick"

Fill in the circle next to the correct answer.

1. Who was sick?

○ Nick

○ Mom

○ the chick

2. What did Mom give Nick?

○ a pet chick

○ a toy chick

○ a big chick

3. Where was Nick?

○ in a tub

○ in a tent

○ in a bed

Draw a line to make a match.

1.    •

   • Nick has a toy chick.

2.    •

   • Nick does not feel sick.

3.    •

   • Nick feels sick.

Write -ick Words

Write the name of the picture on the line.

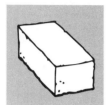

1. _____   2. _____   3. _____

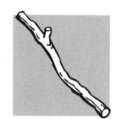

4. _____   5. _____   6. _____

Complete the sentences. Use the words above.

1. Can Nick _____ the ball?

2. Nick has a toy _____.

3. Nick is _____.

4. You can _____ ice cream.

Note: Cut out the slider parts along the dashed lines.
Then slip the word strip through the slider window.

Slide and Read

Pull Up

kick

lick

pick

sick

tick

brick

chick

click

quick

stick

The **-ick** Family

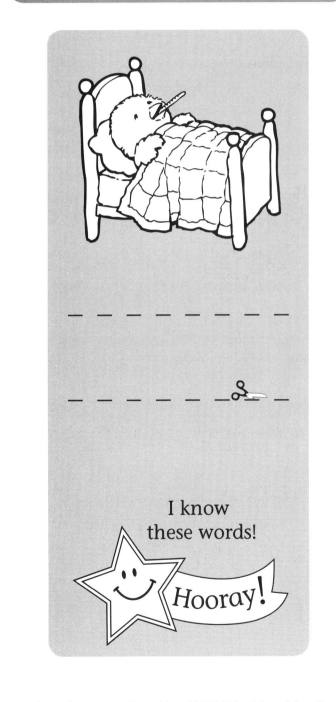

_ _ _ _ _ _ _ _ _

_ _ _ _ _ _ ✂ _

I know
these words!

Hooray!

kick

lick

pick

tick

click

chick

brick

stick

end of
-ick family

lick

tick

click

chick

kick

stick

pick

Meet the **-ill** Word Family

Word Family Practice

Trace the letters. Write **ill** on the lines.
Then sound out the words you wrote.

1.  h <u>i</u> <u>l</u> <u>l</u>

2.  ch ___ ___ ___

3.  gr ___ ___ ___

4.  p ___ ___ ___

5. 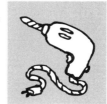 dr ___ ___ ___

6.  sp ___ ___ ___

Story Words to Know

Say each word in the box. Write a word to complete each sentence.
Then read the sentences.

1. I _____ to school.

2. I _____ my lunch.

3. I _____ the table.

> walk
>
> wipe
>
> take

Teacher: Read the story to your students.

Name_____

Teacher: Read the story to your students.

Name _____

Word Family -ill

Listen as the story is read to you.
Underline the words in the **-ill** family.
Then read the story to yourself.

I Will!

"Walk up the hill."
  "I will!"

"Wipe up the spill."
  "I will!"

"Take your pill."
  "I will!"

"I will walk up the hill,
I will wipe up the spill,
I will take my pill."

"I will!
I will!
I will!"

Take the story home. Read the story to your family.

46

Name _____

About "I Will!"

Fill in the circle next to the correct answer.

1. First?

○ walk up the pill

○ walk up the hill

○ walk up the till

2. Next?

○ wipe up the spill

○ wipe up the grill

○ walk up the hill

3. Last?

○ use your drill

○ take your chill

○ take your pill

Draw a line to make a match.

1.  •   • pill

2.  •   • spill

3. •   • hill

Name_____

Write -ill Words

Complete the sentences. Use the words.

> chill   grill   fill   pill

1. Cook the hot dog on the _____.

2. He has a _____.

3. He will _____ the cup.

4. Take your _____.

Write two sentences. Use one word from above in each sentence.

1. _____

_____.

2. _____

_____.

Note: Cut out the slider parts along the dashed lines.
      Then slip the word strip through the slider window.

Slide and Read

↑

Pull Up

fill

hill

pill

will

chill

drill

grill

spill

still

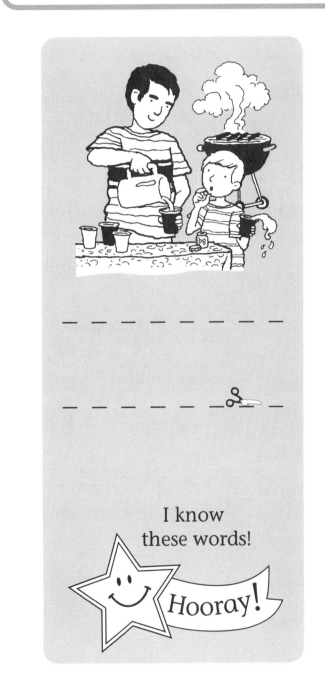

The -ill Family

_ _ _ _ _ _ _ _ _

_ _ _ _ _ _ _ _ ✂ _

I know
these words!

Hooray!

pill

hill

will

chill

drill

drill

end of
-ill family

grill

spill

still

drill

hill

spill

pill

chill

grill

Meet the -ing Word Family

Word Family Practice

Trace the letters. Write **ing** on the lines.
Then sound out the words you wrote.

1.  k <u>i n g</u>

2.  s ____

3.  sw ____

4.  r ____

5.  st ____

6.  w ____

Story Words to Know

Say each word in the box. Write a word to complete each sentence.
Then read the sentences.

1. A bird _____ by me.

2. A _____ has wings.

3. Sit _____ me.

4. _____ you.

bird
by
flew
Thank

Teacher: Read the story to your students.

Name _____

Listen as the story is read to you.
Underline the words in the **-ing** family.
Then read the story to yourself.

King on a Swing

It was a warm spring day.

A king sat on a swing.

Then a bird flew by.

"Will you sing?" asked the king.

The bird did sing.

"Thank you!" said the king.

"I will give you a ring."

The bird put it on her wing.

Take the story home. Read the story to your family.

Name_____

About "King on a Swing"

Fill in the circle next to the correct answer.

1. Who sat on a swing?

  ○ a bird

  ○ a king

  ○ a wing

2. Who did sing?

  ○ a king

  ○ a ring

  ○ a bird

3. Where did the ring go?

  ○ on a swing

  ○ on a wing

  ○ on a string

Which thing would a king sit on?
Circle it.

 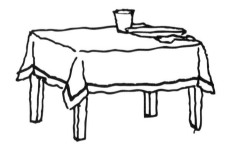 

Name_____

-ing

Write **-ing** Words

Write the name of the picture on the line.

1. _____

2. _____

3. _____

4. _____

5. _____

6. _____

Complete the sentences.
Use the words above.

1. A king fell from a _____.

2. He had to put on a _____.

3. A bee can _____ you.

4. That is a pretty _____.

54   Word Family Stories and Activities • EMC 3354 • © Evan-Moor Corp.

Note: Cut out the slider parts along the dashed lines.
Then slip the word strip through the slider window.

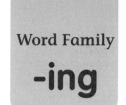

Word Family
-ing

Slide and Read

↑

Pull Up

king

ring

sing

wing

bring

spring

sting

string

swing

The **-ing** Family

I know
these words!

Hooray!

king

sing

ring

bring

sting

wing

end of
-ing family

ring

swing

king

string

sing

swing

wing

bring

sting

Meet the **-ink** Word Family

Word Family Practice

Trace the letters. Write **ink** on the lines.
Then sound out the words you wrote.

1.  m <u>i n k</u>

2.  w _ _ _

3.  dr _ _ _

4.  s _ _ _

5.  p _ _ _

6.  shr _ _ _

Story Words to Know

Say each word in the box. Write a word to complete each sentence.
Then read the sentences.

1. I _____ a pet.

2. _____ I cry.

3. Don't _____.

4. She _____ have one.

| Sometimes |
| have |
| doesn't |
| worry |

Teacher: Read the story to your students.

Name _____

Listen as the story is read to you.
Underline the words in the -**ink** family.
Then read the story to yourself.

My Mink

I have a pet mink.

Sometimes he can stink.
I wash him in the sink.
Don't worry, he doesn't shrink.

I give him water to drink.
I show him how to wink.

Pet minks are fun.
Maybe you'd like one?

What do you think?

Take the story home. Read the story to your family.

Word Family Stories and Activities • EMC 3354 • © Evan-Moor Corp.

Name_____

About "My Mink"

Fill in the circle next to the correct answer.

1. Sometimes the pet mink can _____.
- ○ pink
- ○ stink
- ○ blink

2. The pet mink gets washed in _____.
- ○ the sink
- ○ the drink
- ○ the pink

3. The girl shows him how to _____.
- ○ shrink
- ○ drink
- ○ wink

Yes or no?
Circle the answer.

1. Can you wink?

yes   no

2. Do you wash in the sink?

yes   no

Name _____

Write **-ink** Words

Complete the sentences.
Use the words.

> drink   Pink   sink   stink

1. I will get a _____.

2. I wash dishes in the _____.

3. _____ is a color.

4. Yuck! You _____!

Find the word that matches the picture.
Circle it.

1.    stink   shrink

2.    sink   wink

3.    link   pink

Note: Cut out the slider parts along the dashed lines.
Then slip the word strip through the slider window.

Slide and Read

Pull Up

link

mink

pink

rink

sink

wink

blink

drink

shrink

stink

The **-ink** Family

I know
these words!

Hooray!

mink

pink

link

rink

sink

end of
-ink family

wink

blink

drink

link

shrink

mink

sink

stink

pink

rink

Meet the **-ock** Word Family

Word Family Practice

Trace the letters. Write **ock** on the lines.
Then sound out the words you wrote.

1.  l <u>o c k</u>

2. 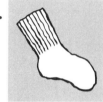 s _ _ _

3.  bl _ _ _

4.  r _ _ _

5.  cl _ _ _

6.  sm _ _ _

Story Words to Know

Say each word in the box. Write a word to complete each sentence.
Then read the sentences.

1. I _____ Kim a rock.

2. What is _____ the box?

3. That is a _____ bird.

gave

little

inside

Name _____

Listen as the story is read to you.
Underline the words in the **-ock** family.
Then read the story to yourself.

The Box

Kim saw a box with a lock.

She gave the box a knock with a rock.

Then she had a shock!

Inside the box Kim saw…

a little blue sock,

a little tick-tock clock,

a little toy block,

And her old smock.

It was Kim's baby box!

Take the story home. Read the story to your family.

64   Word Family Stories and Activities • EMC 3354 • © Evan-Moor Corp.

Name_____

About "The Box"

Fill in the circle next to the correct answer.

1. How did Kim get the lock off?
   - ○ She gave it a knock with a rock.
   - ○ She gave it a knock with a block.
   - ○ She gave it a rock with a sock.

2. What was one item in the box?
   - ○ a tick-tock clock
   - ○ a little rock
   - ○ a pretty frock

3. What was <u>not</u> in the box?
   - ○ a tick-tock clock
   - ○ a little toy block
   - ○ a pretty frock

Draw a line to make a match.

1.

2.

3.

• lock

• sock

• clock

Name_____

Write **-ock** Words

Complete the sentences.
Use the words.

block   dock   rock   sock

1. The boat was at the _____ .

2. I tied it to a big _____ .

3. Where is my other _____ ?

4. There is a **G** on the toy _____ .

Look at each picture.
Write a sentence about it.

1.  _____

_____ .

2.  _____

_____ .

Slide and Read

Pull Up

dock

lock

rock

sock

block

clock

frock

knock

smock

The **-ock** Family

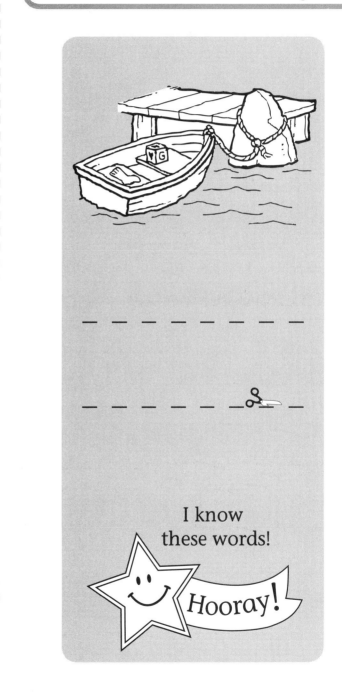

I know
these words!

Hooray!

EMC 3354 • © Evan-Moor Corp.

Word Family Stories and Activities • EMC 3354 • © Evan-Moor Corp.

dock

lock

rock

sock

clock

knock

end of
-ock family

frock

smock

rock

sock

dock

clock

lock

smock

knock

Meet the -og Word Family

Word Family Practice

Trace the letters. Write **og** on the lines.
Then sound out the words you wrote.

1.  d o g

2.  fr __ __

3.  j __ __

4.  f __ __

5.  h __ __

6.  l __ __

Story Words to Know

Say each word in the box. Write a word to complete each sentence.
Then read the sentences.

1. A hog _____ a dog.

2. _____ went for a jog.

3. They got _____ in the fog.

saw
lost
They

Name _____

Listen as the story is read to you.
Underline the words in the **-og** family.
Then read the story to yourself.

A Jog in the Fog

A dog went for a jog.

He met a hog.

"May I jog with you?" asked the hog.

"You may!" said the dog.

They got lost in the fog.

"Where are we?" asked the dog.

"I don't know," said the hog.

Then they saw a frog on a log.

"I can get you out of the fog!" said the frog.

So the dog, the hog, and the frog all went for a jog.

Take the story home. Read the story to your family.

Word Family Stories and Activities • EMC 3354 • © Evan-Moor Corp.

Name_____

About "A Jog in the Fog"

Fill in the circle next to the correct answer.

1. First?
- ○ A dog went for a jog.
- ○ A frog went for a jog.
- ○ A hog went for a jog.

2. Next?
- ○ A dog and a frog went for a jog.
- ○ A frog and a hog went for a jog.
- ○ A hog and a dog went for a jog.

3. Last?
- ○ A dog, a hog, and a frog went for a jog.
- ○ A frog went for a jog.
- ○ A frog got lost in the fog.

Yes or no?
Circle the answer.

1. Did the frog jog?

yes   no

2. Was the dog on a log?

yes   no

Name _____

Write **-og** Words

Complete the sentences.
Use the words.

| dog   fog   jog   log |

1. I have a _____.

2. We went for a _____.

3. We got lost in the _____.

4. I fell over a _____.

Find the word that matches the picture.
Circle it.

1.    flog   log

2.   hog   hot

3.    fog   frog

Note: Cut out the slider parts along the dashed lines.
      Then slip the word strip through the slider window.

Slide and Read

Pull Up

dog

fog

hog

jog

log

clog

frog

smog

The **-og** Family

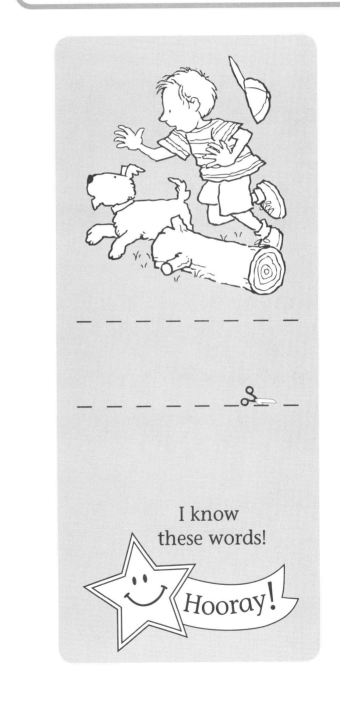

I know
these words!

Hooray!

EMC 3354 • © Evan-Moor Corp.

Word Family Stories and Activities • EMC 3354 • © Evan-Moor Corp.

fog

dog

hog

jog

log

frog

end of -og family

clog

smog

hog

jog

fog

dog

log

smog

frog

Name_____

Meet the -um Word Family

Word Family Practice

Trace the letters. Write **um** on the lines.
Then sound out the words you wrote.

1.  d r u m

2.  pl __ __

3.  g __ __

4.  h __ __

5.  ch __ __

6.  sw __ __

Story Words to Know

Say each word in the box. Write a word to complete each sentence.
Then read the sentences.

1. I like to _____ gum.

2. Can you _____ over today?

3. We are _____ ten years old.

4. I know how to _____ a drum.

play

chew

both

come

Name _____

Listen as the story is read to you.
Underline the words in the **-um** family.
Then read the story. to yourself.

My Chum and Me

I have a chum.

He can play the drum.

I can hum.

When I hum, he plays the drum.

We both chew gum.

Can you hum?

Can you play the drum?

Can you chew gum?

Come play with my chum and me.

Name _____

About "My Chum and Me"

Fill in the circle next to the correct answer.

1. The boy can _____.
   - ○ drum
   - ○ hum
   - ○ gum

2. His chum can play _____.
   - ○ the drum
   - ○ the plum
   - ○ the hum

3. They can both chew _____.
   - ○ drum
   - ○ gum
   - ○ plum

What can you eat in the **-um** word family?
Circle them.

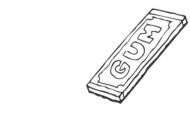

Name _____

Write **-um** Words

Write the name of the picture on the line.

1. _____

2. _____

3. _____

4. _____

5. _____

6. _____

Complete the sentences.
Use the words above.

1. He ate a big _____.

2. Then, he tried to _____.

3. Next, he hit a _____.

4. Then, he chewed some _____.

Note: Cut out the slider parts along the dashed lines.
Then slip the word strip through the slider window.

Slide and Read

Pull Up

hum

gum

sum

chum

drum

plum

swum

strum

The -um Family

I know
these words!

Hooray!

Word Family Stories and Activities • EMC 3354 • © Evan-Moor Corp.

gum

hum

sum

chum

drum

plum

end of
-um family

swum

strum

hum

drum

gum

sum

chum

strum

plum

Name_____

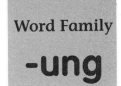
Meet the **-ung** Word Family

Word Family Practice

Trace the letters. Write **ung** on the lines.
Then sound out the words you wrote.

1.  h u n g

2.  l _ _ _

3. 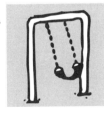 sw _ _ _

4.  fl _ _ _

5.  s _ _ _

6.  st _ _ _

Story Words to Know

Say each word in the box. Write a word to complete each sentence.
Then read the sentences.

1. I like to go to _____.

2. It is so _____ at night.

3. I go home _____ school.

after

quiet

school

Name_____

Listen as the story is read to you.
Underline the words in the -**ung** family.
Then read the story to yourself.

After School

It is quiet after school.

The last bell has rung.

The last swing has swung.

The last ball has been flung.

The last song has been sung.

Every coat is hung.

It is so quiet after school!

Take the story home. Read the story to your family.

82

Word Family Stories and Activities • EMC 3354 • © Evan-Moor Corp.

About "After School"

Fill in the circle next to the correct answer.

1. The last song _____.
   ○ has been sung
   ○ is hung up
   ○ has rung

2. The last bell has _____.
   ○ sung
   ○ rung
   ○ hung

3. The last ball has _____.
   ○ been flung
   ○ swung
   ○ rung

Yes or no?
Circle the answer.

1. Do you go to school?

yes   no

2. Do you play outside after school?

yes   no

Name _____

Write **-ung** Words

Complete the sentences.
Use the words.

| clung | hung | stung | swung |

1. I _____ up my coat.

2. A bee _____ to my coat.

3. I _____ at the bee.

4. The bee _____ me!

Find the word that matches the picture.
Circle it.

1. 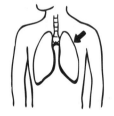   stung   lung

2.    flung   hung

3.    swung   sung

Word Family Stories and Activities • EMC 3354 • © Evan-Moor Corp.

Note: Cut out the slider parts along the dashed lines.
Then slip the word strip through the slider window.

Slide and Read

Pull Up

hung

lung

rung

sung

clung

flung

sprung

swung

The **-ung** Family

I know
these words!

Hooray!

rung

hung

lung

sung

flung

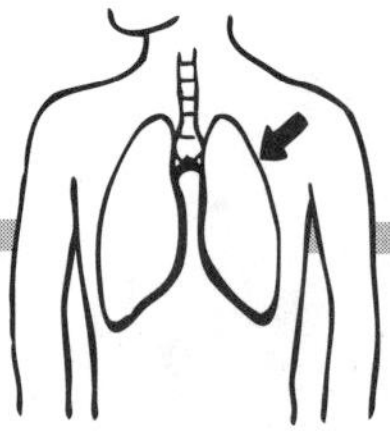

sprung

end of
-ung family

swung

lung

rung

sprung

flung

swung

hung

sung

flung

Meet the -unk Word Family

Trace the letters. Write **unk** on the lines.
Then sound out the words you wrote.

1.  bu n k

2.  s _ _ _

3.  tr _ _ _

4.  d _ _ _

5.  sk _ _ _

6.  j _ _ _

Say each word in the box. Write a word to complete each sentence.
Then read the sentences.

1. I love to eat _____.

2. I wear a _____ when it is cold.

3. There are a lot of _____ to see.

things

sweater

chocolate

Name _____

Listen as the story is read to you.
Underline the words in the **-unk** family.
Then read the story to yourself.

The Junk Sale

Dad and I went to a junk sale.

We saw a lot of things…

a pretty trunk,

a toy skunk,

a sweater that shrunk,

a bed to bunk,

a boat that sunk,

and a chocolate chunk.

It sure is fun to look at junk!

Take the story home. Read the story to your family.

Word Family Stories and Activities • EMC 3354 • © Evan-Moor Corp.

Name_____

About "The Junk Sale"

Fill in the circle next to the correct answer.

1. There was a toy _____.
- ○ shrunk
- ○ skunk
- ○ sunk

2. The bed was _____.
- ○ a hunk
- ○ a trunk
- ○ a bunk

3. There was a chocolate _____.
- ○ chunk
- ○ trunk
- ○ stunk

Draw a line to make a match.

1. •   • trunk

2.  •   • bunk

3.  •   • skunk

Name_____

Write **-unk** Words

Complete the sentences.
Use the words.

> chunk   junk   sunk   trunk

1. I went to a _____ sale.

2. I got a pretty _____.

3. I got a big _____ of rock.

4. The sun had not _____ yet.

_____

Look at each picture.
Write a sentence about it.

1.  _____

   _____.

2.  _____

   _____.

Note: Cut out the slider parts along the dashed lines.
Then slip the word strip through the slider window.

Slide and Read

Pull Up

bunk

dunk

junk

sunk

chunk

clunk

shrunk

skunk

stunk

trunk

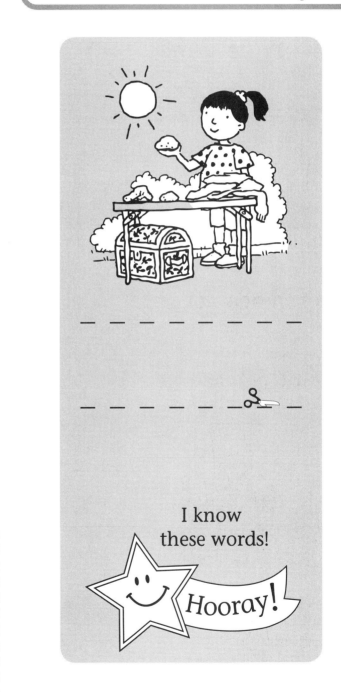

The **-unk** Family

_ _ _ _ _ _ _ _ _

_ _ _ _ _ _ ✂ _

I know
these words!

Hooray!

bunk

junk

sunk

chunk

clunk

end of
-unk family

skunk

shrunk

stunk

trunk

clunk

junk

sunk

chunk

skunk

shrunk

Name _____

Meet the **-ush** Word Family

Word Family Practice

Trace the letters. Write **ush** on the lines.
Then sound out the words you wrote.

1.  fl u s h

2.  m ____ ____ ____

3.  cr ____ ____ ____

4.  r ____ ____ ____

5.  br ____ ____ ____

6.  bl ____ ____ ____

Story Words to Know

Say each word in the box. Write a word to complete each sentence.
Then read the sentences.

1. _____ shut the door.

2. Don't forget to say _____.

3. I _____ go home now.

Please

must

good-bye

Name _____

Listen as the story is read to you.
Underline the words in the **-ush** family.
Then read the story to yourself.

I Can

Please do not gush.

Please do not blush.

But I must tell you everything I can do.

I can flush.

I can brush.

I can crush.

I can hush.

And I can rush.

Now I must go eat my mush.

Good-bye!

Take the story home. Read the story to your family.

Name _____

About "I Can"

Fill in the circle next to the correct answer.

1. Please do not _____.
- ○ gush
- ○ slush
- ○ flush

2. He can _____.
- ○ slush
- ○ hush
- ○ mush

3. The boy must go eat his _____.
- ○ slush
- ○ mush
- ○ brush

What can you do?
Circle it.

Name _____

Write **-ush** Words

Write the name of the picture on the line.

1. _____

2. _____

3. _____

4. _____

5. _____

6. _____

Complete the sentences.
Use the words above.

1. There is no more _____ in my bowl.

2. Mom will _____ the can.

3. The girl had to _____ off.

4. Did I make you _____?

Note: Cut out the slider parts along the dashed lines.
Then slip the word strip through the slider window.

Slide and Read

Pull Up

hush

gush

mush

rush

blush

brush

crush

flush

plush

The **-ush** Family

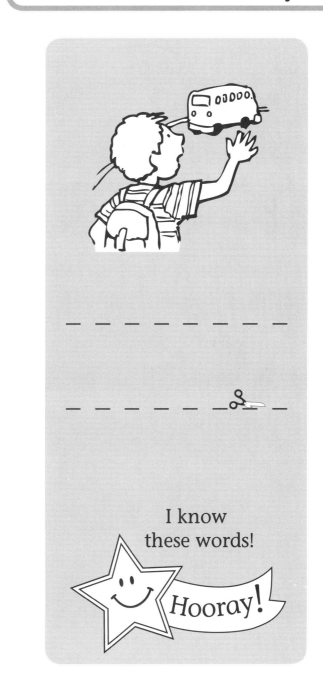

_ _ _ _ _ _ _ _ _

_ _ _ _ _ _ _ ✂ _

I know
these words!

Hooray!

Word Family Stories and Activities • EMC 3354 • © Evan-Moor Corp.

gush

rush

hush

blush

brush

mush

end of
-ush family

crush

flush

gush

mush

brush

plush

hush

flush

crush

Answer Key

Page 3

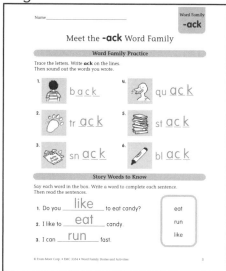

Page 4

Page 5

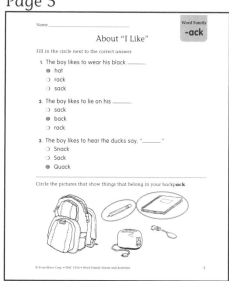

Page 6

Page 9

Page 10

Page 11

Name_____

About "It Is Grand"

Word Family
-and

Fill in the circle next to the correct answer.

1. It is grand to listen _____.
   ○ in the sand
   ● to the band
   ○ on your hand

2. It is grand to play _____.
   ● in the sand
   ○ to the band
   ○ a command

3. It is grand to stand on your _____.
   ○ sand
   ○ band
   ● hand

Yes or no?
Circle the answer.   Answers may vary.

1. Have you ever played in the sand?   ☺ yes   ☹ no

2. Can you stand on your hand?   ☺ yes   ☹ no

© Evan-Moor Corp. • EMC 3354 • Word Family Stories and Activities   11

Page 12

Name_____

Write -and Words

Word Family
-and

Complete the sentences.
Use the words.

hand   sand   land   stand

1. I can play in the ___sand___
2. My ___hand___ hurts.
3. Dogs live on ___land___
4. The baby can ___stand___

Find the word that matches the picture.
Circle it.

1. (grand)   land
2. sand   (band)
3. stand   (hand)

12   Word Family Stories and Activities • EMC 3354 • © Evan-Moor Corp.

Page 15

Name_____

Meet the -atch Word Family

Word Family
-atch

Word Family Practice

Trace the letters. Write **atch** on the lines.
Then sound out the words you wrote.

1. c a t c h
2. m atch
3. p atch
4. h atch
5. l atch
6. scr atch

Story Words to Know

Say each word in the box. Write a word to complete each sentence.
Then read the sentences.

1. It is ___hard___ to stand on one foot.
2. The hen lives in a big ___house___
3. My dog ___waits___ for me at the bus stop.

henhouse
waits
hard

© Evan-Moor Corp. • EMC 3354 • Word Family Stories and Activities   15

Page 16

Teacher: Read the story to your students.

Name_____

Word Family
-atch

Listen as the story is read to you.
Underline the words in the -atch family.
Then read the story to yourself.

Scratch

I have a hen.

I call her Scratch.

Scratch can run fast.

She is hard to catch!

Scratch runs into her henhouse.

And I close the latch.

She sits on her eggs and waits for them to hatch.

Crack, crack, crack!

1, 2, 3, chicks that match!

You are a mama now, Scratch!

Take the story home. Read the story to your family.

16   Word Family Stories and Activities • EMC 3354 • © Evan-Moor Corp.

Page 17

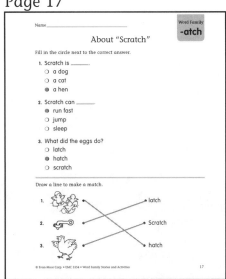

Name_____

About "Scratch"

Word Family
-atch

Fill in the circle next to the correct answer.

1. Scratch is _____.
   ○ a dog
   ○ a cat
   ● a hen

2. Scratch can _____.
   ● run fast
   ○ jump
   ○ sleep

3. What did the eggs do?
   ○ latch
   ● hatch
   ○ scratch

Draw a line to make a match.

1. • latch
2. • Scratch
3. • hatch

© Evan-Moor Corp. • EMC 3354 • Word Family Stories and Activities   17

Page 18

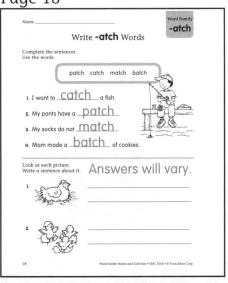

Name_____

Write -atch Words

Word Family
-atch

Complete the sentences.
Use the words.

patch   catch   match   batch

1. I want to ___catch___ a fish.
2. My pants have a ___patch___
3. My socks do not ___match___
4. Mom made a ___batch___ of cookies.

Look at each picture.
Write a sentence about it.   Answers will vary.

1. _____
2. _____

18   Word Family Stories and Activities • EMC 3354 • © Evan-Moor Corp.

Page 21

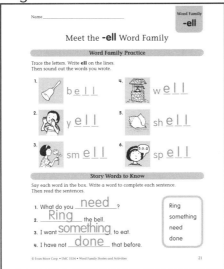

Name_____

Word Family **-ell**

Meet the **-ell** Word Family

Word Family Practice

Trace the letters. Write **ell** on the lines.
Then sound out the words you wrote.

1. b e l l
2. y e l l
3. sm e l l
4. w e l l
5. sh e l l
6. sp e l l

Story Words to Know

Say each word in the box. Write a word to complete each sentence.
Then read the sentences.

1. What do you _need_ ?
2. _Ring_ the bell.
3. I want _something_ to eat.
4. I have not _done_ that before.

Ring
something
need
done

© Evan-Moor Corp. • EMC 3354 • Word Family Stories and Activities   21

Page 22

Teacher: Read the story to your students.
Name_____

Word Family **-ell**

Listen as the story is read to you.
Underline the words in the **-ell** family.
Then read the story to yourself.

Just Tell Nell!

Do you need something done?

Just tell Nell!

Tell Nell to ring the bell.

Tell Nell to find a shell.

Tell Nell to smell.

Tell Nell to yell.

Tell Nell to spell.

Do you need something done?

Just tell Nell!

Take the story home. Read the story to your family.

22   Word Family Stories and Activities • EMC 3354 • © Evan-Moor Corp.

Page 23

Name_____

Word Family **-ell**

About "Just Tell Nell!"

Fill in the circle next to the correct answer.

1. Tell Nell to ring _____
   ● the bell
   ○ the smell
   ○ the yell

2. Tell Nell to find _____
   ○ a bell
   ● a shell
   ○ a well

3. Do you need something done?
   ○ Just yell!
   ○ Just smell!
   ● Just tell Nell!

Which things smell good?
Circle the pictures.

© Evan-Moor Corp. • EMC 3354 • Word Family Stories and Activities   23

Page 24

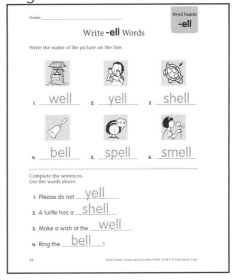

Name_____

Word Family **-ell**

Write **-ell** Words

Write the name of the picture on the line.

1. well
2. yell
3. shell
4. bell
5. spell
6. smell

Complete the sentences.
Use the words above.

1. Please do not _yell_
2. A turtle has a _shell_
3. Make a wish at the _well_
4. Ring the _bell_

24   Word Family Stories and Activities • EMC 3354 • © Evan-Moor Corp.

Page 27

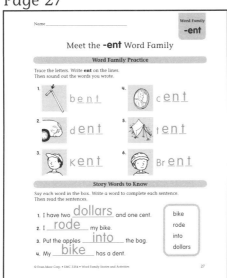

Name_____

Word Family **-ent**

Meet the **-ent** Word Family

Word Family Practice

Trace the letters. Write **ent** on the lines.
Then sound out the words you wrote.

1. b e n t
2. d e n t
3. k e n t
4. c e n t
5. t e n t
6. Br e n t

Story Words to Know

Say each word in the box. Write a word to complete each sentence.
Then read the sentences.

1. I have two _dollars_ and one cent.
2. I _rode_ my bike.
3. Put the apples _into_ the bag.
4. My _bike_ has a dent.

bike
rode
into
dollars

© Evan-Moor Corp. • EMC 3354 • Word Family Stories and Activities   27

Page 28

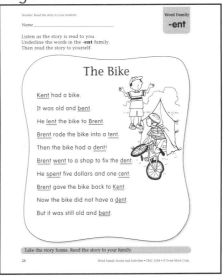

Teacher: Read the story to your students.
Name_____

Word Family **-ent**

Listen as the story is read to you.
Underline the words in the **-ent** family.
Then read the story to yourself.

The Bike

Kent had a bike.

It was old and bent.

He lent the bike to Brent.

Brent rode the bike into a tent.

Then the bike had a dent!

Brent went to a shop to fix the dent.

He spent five dollars and one cent.

Brent gave the bike back to Kent.

Now the bike did not have a dent.

But it was still old and bent.

Take the story home. Read the story to your family.

28   Word Family Stories and Activities • EMC 3354 • © Evan-Moor Corp.

Page 29

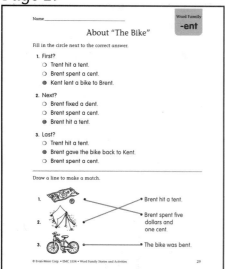

Name_____

Word Family -ent

About "The Bike"

Fill in the circle next to the correct answer.

1. First?
   ○ Trent hit a tent.
   ○ Brent spent a cent.
   ● Kent lent a bike to Brent.

2. Next?
   ○ Brent fixed a dent.
   ○ Brent spent a cent.
   ● Brent hit a tent.

3. Last?
   ○ Trent hit a tent.
   ● Brent gave the bike back to Kent.
   ○ Brent spent a cent.

Draw a line to make a match.

1. (dollar) — Brent hit a tent.
2. (tent) — Brent spent five dollars and one cent.
3. (bike) — The bike was bent.

© Evan-Moor Corp. • EMC 3354 • Word Family Stories and Activities   29

Page 30

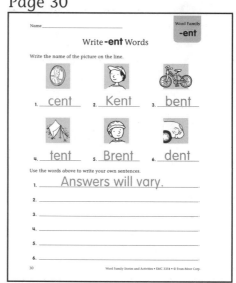

Name_____

Word Family -ent

Write -ent Words

Write the name of the picture on the line.

1. cent   2. Kent   3. bent
4. tent   5. Brent   6. dent

Use the words above to write your own sentences.

1. _Answers will vary._
2. _____
3. _____
4. _____
5. _____
6. _____

30   Word Family Stories and Activities • EMC 3354 • © Evan-Moor Corp.

Page 33

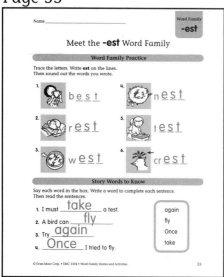

Name_____

Word Family -est

Meet the -est Word Family

Word Family Practice

Trace the letters. Write **est** on the lines.
Then sound out the words you wrote.

1. best   4. nest
2. rest   5. test
3. west   6. crest

Story Words to Know

Say each word in the box. Write a word to complete each sentence.
Then read the sentences.

1. I must _take_ a test.
2. A bird can _fly_ .
3. Try _again_ .
4. _Once_ I tried to fly.

| again |
| fly |
| Once |
| take |

© Evan-Moor Corp. • EMC 3354 • Word Family Stories and Activities   33

Page 34

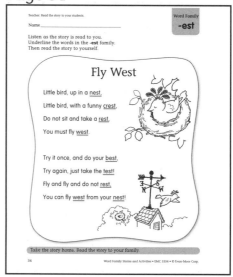

Teacher: Read the story to your students.

Name_____

Word Family -est

Listen as the story is read to you.
Underline the words in the -est family.
Then read the story to yourself.

Fly West

Little bird, up in a <u>nest</u>,
Little bird, with a funny <u>crest</u>,
Do not sit and take a <u>rest</u>.
You must fly <u>west</u>.

Try it once, and do your <u>best</u>,
Try again, just take the <u>test</u>!
Fly and fly and do not <u>rest</u>,
You can fly <u>west</u> from your <u>nest</u>!

Take the story home. Read the story to your family.

34   Word Family Stories and Activities • EMC 3354 • © Evan-Moor Corp.

Page 35

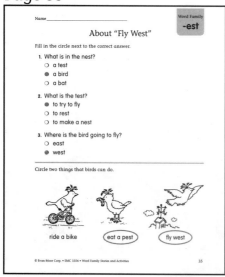

Name_____

Word Family -est

About "Fly West"

Fill in the circle next to the correct answer.

1. What is in the nest?
   ○ a test
   ● a bird
   ○ a bat

2. What is the test?
   ● to try to fly
   ○ to rest
   ○ to make a nest

3. Where is the bird going to fly?
   ○ east
   ● west

Circle two things that birds can do.

ride a bike   eat a pest   fly west

© Evan-Moor Corp. • EMC 3354 • Word Family Stories and Activities   35

Page 36

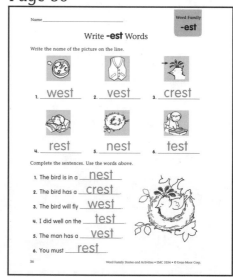

Name_____

Word Family -est

Write -est Words

Write the name of the picture on the line.

1. west   2. vest   3. crest
4. rest   5. nest   6. test

Complete the sentences. Use the words above.

1. The bird is in a _nest_ .
2. The bird has a _crest_ .
3. The bird will fly _west_ .
4. I did well on the _test_ .
5. The man has a _vest_ .
6. You must _rest_ .

36   Word Family Stories and Activities • EMC 3354 • © Evan-Moor Corp.

Page 39

Page 40

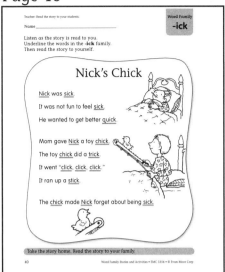

Page 41

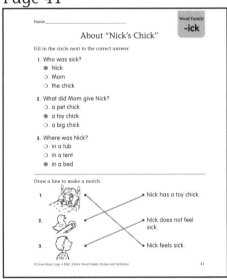

Page 42

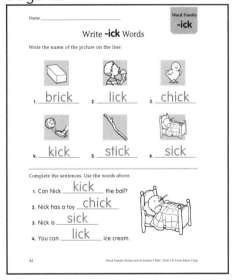

Page 45

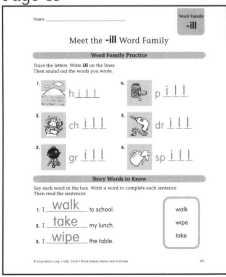

Page 46

Page 47

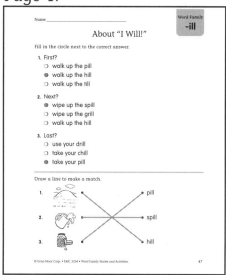

Page 48

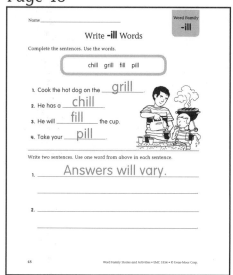

Page 51

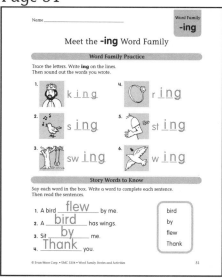

Page 52

Page 53

Page 54

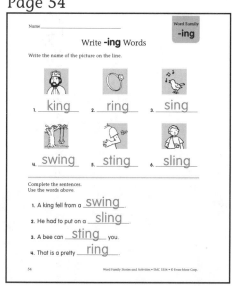

Word Family Stories and Activities • EMC 3354 • © Evan-Moor Corp.

Page 57

Name _____

Word Family **-ink**

Meet the **-ink** Word Family

Word Family Practice

Trace the letters. Write **ink** on the lines.
Then sound out the words you wrote.

1. m i n k
2. w i n k
3. dr i n k
4. s i n k
5. p i n k
6. shr i n k

Story Words to Know

Say each word in the box. Write a word to complete each sentence.
Then read the sentences.

1. I _have_ a pet.
2. _Sometimes_ I cry.
3. Don't _worry_
4. She _doesn't_ have one.

Sometimes
have
doesn't
worry

© Evan-Moor Corp. • EMC 3354 • Word Family Stories and Activities   57

Page 58

Teacher: Read the story to your students.

Name _____

Word Family **-ink**

Listen as the story is read to you.
Underline the words in the **-ink** family.
Then read the story to yourself.

My Mink

I have a pet mink.

Sometimes he can stink.
I wash him in the sink.
Don't worry, he doesn't shrink.

I give him water to drink.
I show him how to wink.

Pet minks are fun.
Maybe you'd like one?

What do you think?

Take the story home. Read the story to your family.

58   Word Family Stories and Activities • EMC 3354 • © Evan-Moor Corp.

Page 59

Name _____

Word Family **-ink**

About "My Mink"

Fill in the circle next to the correct answer.

1. Sometimes the pet mink can _____.
   ○ pink
   ● stink
   ○ blink

2. The pet mink gets washed in _____.
   ● the sink
   ○ the drink
   ○ the pink

3. The girl shows him how to _____.
   ○ shrink
   ○ drink
   ● wink

Yes or no?   **Answers will vary.**
Circle the answer.

1. Can you wink?   ☺ yes   ☹ no

2. Do you wash in the sink?   ☺ yes   ☹ no

© Evan-Moor Corp. • EMC 3354 • Word Family Stories and Activities   59

Page 60

Name _____

Word Family **-ink**

Write **-ink** Words

Complete the sentences.
Use the words.

drink   Pink   sink   stink

1. I will get a _drink_
2. I wash dishes in the _sink_
3. _Pink_ is a color.
4. Yuck! You _stink_

Find the word that matches the picture.
Circle it.

1. stink   (shrink)
2. sink   (wink)
3. (link)   pink

60   Word Family Stories and Activities • EMC 3354 • © Evan-Moor Corp.

Page 63

Name _____

Word Family **-ock**

Meet the **-ock** Word Family

Word Family Practice

Trace the letters. Write **ock** on the lines.
Then sound out the words you wrote.

1. l o c k
2. s o c k
3. bl o c k
4. r o c k
5. cl o c k
6. sm o c k

Story Words to Know

Say each word in the box. Write a word to complete each sentence.
Then read the sentences.

1. I _gave_ Kim a rock.
2. What is _inside_ the box?
3. That is a _little_ bird.

gave
little
inside

© Evan-Moor Corp. • EMC 3354 • Word Family Stories and Activities   63

Page 64

Teacher: Read the story to your students.

Name _____

Word Family **-ock**

Listen as the story is read to you.
Underline the words in the **-ock** family.
Then read the story to yourself.

The Box

Kim saw a box with a lock.
She gave the box a knock with a rock.
Then she had a shock!

Inside the box Kim saw…

a little blue sock,

a little tick-tock clock,

a little toy block.

And her old smock.

It was Kim's baby box!

Take the story home. Read the story to your family.

64   Word Family Stories and Activities • EMC 3354 • © Evan-Moor Corp.

Page 65

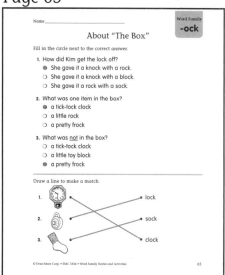

Name_____

About "The Box"

Word Family **-ock**

Fill in the circle next to the correct answer.

1. How did Kim get the lock off?
   - ● She gave it a knock with a rock.
   - ○ She gave it a knock with a block.
   - ○ She gave it a rock with a sock.

2. What was one item in the box?
   - ● a tick-tock clock
   - ○ a little rock
   - ○ a pretty frock

3. What was not in the box?
   - ○ a tick-tock clock
   - ○ a little toy block
   - ● a pretty frock

Draw a line to make a match.

1. clock
2. lock
3. sock

© Evan-Moor Corp. • EMC 3354 • Word Family Stories and Activities   65

Page 66

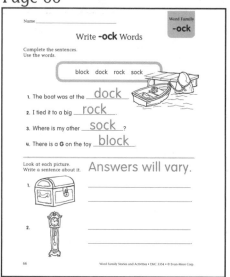

Name_____

Write **-ock** Words

Word Family **-ock**

Complete the sentences.
Use the words.

block dock rock sock

1. The boat was at the __dock__
2. I tied it to a big __rock__
3. Where is my other __sock__?
4. There is a **G** on the toy __block__

Look at each picture.
Write a sentence about it.   Answers will vary.

1.
2.

66   Word Family Stories and Activities • EMC 3354 • © Evan-Moor Corp.

Page 69

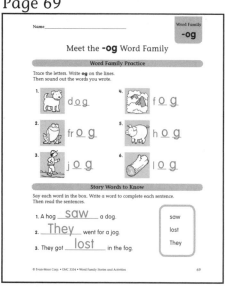

Name_____

Meet the **-og** Word Family

Word Family **-og**

Word Family Practice

Trace the letters. Write **og** on the lines.
Then sound out the words you wrote.

1. d o g
2. fr o g
3. j o g
4. f o g
5. h o g
6. l o g

Story Words to Know

Say each word in the box. Write a word to complete each sentence.
Then read the sentences.

1. A hog __saw__ a dog.
2. __They__ went for a jog.
3. They got __lost__ in the fog.

saw
lost
They

© Evan-Moor Corp. • EMC 3354 • Word Family Stories and Activities   69

Page 70

Teacher: Read the story to your students.

Name_____

Word Family **-og**

Listen as the story is read to you.
Underline the words in the **-og** family.
Then read the story to yourself.

A Jog in the Fog

A dog went for a jog.
He met a hog.
"May I jog with you?" asked the hog.
"You may!" said the dog.
They got lost in the fog.

"Where are we?" asked the dog.
"I don't know," said the hog.
Then they saw a frog on a log.
"I can get you out of the fog!" said the frog.
So the dog, the hog, and the frog all went for a jog.

Take the story home. Read the story to your family.

70   Word Family Stories and Activities • EMC 3354 • © Evan-Moor Corp.

Page 71

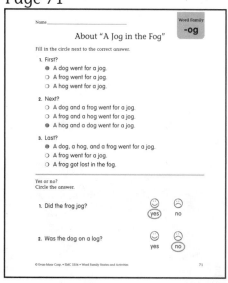

Name_____

About "A Jog in the Fog"

Word Family **-og**

Fill in the circle next to the correct answer.

1. First?
   - ● A dog went for a jog.
   - ○ A frog went for a jog.
   - ○ A hog went for a jog.

2. Next?
   - ○ A dog and a frog went for a jog.
   - ○ A frog and a hog went for a jog.
   - ● A hog and a dog went for a jog.

3. Last?
   - ● A dog, a hog, and frog went for a jog.
   - ○ A frog went for a jog.
   - ○ A frog got lost in the fog.

Yes or no?
Circle the answer.

1. Did the frog jog?   yes   no   (yes)

2. Was the dog on a log?   yes   no   (no)

© Evan-Moor Corp. • EMC 3354 • Word Family Stories and Activities   71

Page 72

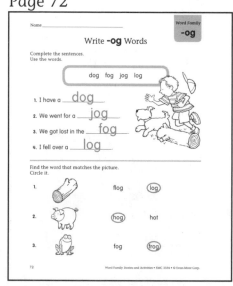

Name_____

Write **-og** Words

Word Family **-og**

Complete the sentences.
Use the words.

dog fog jog log

1. I have a __dog__
2. We went for a __jog__
3. We got lost in the __fog__
4. I fell over a __log__

Find the word that matches the picture.
Circle it.

1.   flog   (log)
2.   (hog)   hot
3.   fog   (frog)

72   Word Family Stories and Activities • EMC 3354 • © Evan-Moor Corp.

Page 75

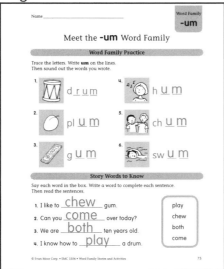

Word Family
-um

Meet the **-um** Word Family

Word Family Practice

Trace the letters. Write **um** on the lines.
Then sound out the words you wrote.

1. d r u m
2. pl u m
3. g u m
4. h u m
5. ch u m
6. sw u m

Story Words to Know

Say each word in the box. Write a word to complete each sentence.
Then read the sentences.

1. I like to **chew** gum.
2. Can you **come** over today?
3. We are **both** ten years old.
4. I know how to **play** a drum.

play
chew
both
come

© Evan-Moor Corp. • EMC 3354 • Word Family Stories and Activities   75

Page 76

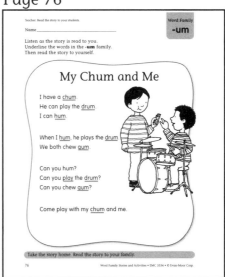

Teacher: Read the story to your students.
Name_____

Word Family
-um

Listen as the story is read to you.
Underline the words in the **-um** family.
Then read the story to yourself.

My Chum and Me

I have a chum.
He can play the drum.
I can hum.

When I hum, he plays the drum.
We both chew gum.

Can you hum?
Can you play the drum?
Can you chew gum?

Come play with my chum and me.

Take the story home. Read the story to your family.

76   Word Family Stories and Activities • EMC 3354 • © Evan-Moor Corp.

Page 77

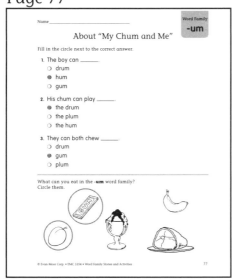

Name_____

Word Family
-um

About "My Chum and Me"

Fill in the circle next to the correct answer.

1. The boy can _____.
   ○ drum
   ● hum
   ○ gum

2. His chum can play _____.
   ● the drum
   ○ the plum
   ○ the hum

3. They can both chew _____.
   ○ drum
   ● gum
   ○ plum

What can you eat in the **-um** word family?
Circle them.

© Evan-Moor Corp. • EMC 3354 • Word Family Stories and Activities   77

Page 78

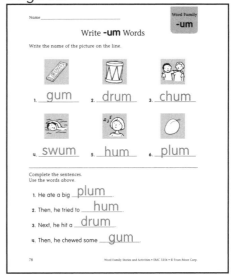

Name_____

Word Family
-um

Write **-um** Words

Write the name of the picture on the line.

1. gum
2. drum
3. chum
4. swum
5. hum
6. plum

Complete the sentences.
Use the words above.

1. He ate a big **plum**.
2. Then, he tried to **hum**.
3. Next, he hit a **drum**.
4. Then, he chewed some **gum**.

78   Word Family Stories and Activities • EMC 3354 • © Evan-Moor Corp.

Page 81

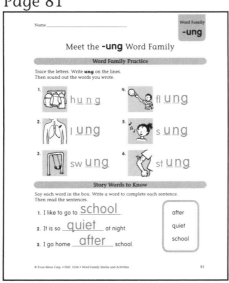

Name_____

Word Family
-ung

Meet the **-ung** Word Family

Word Family Practice

Trace the letters. Write **ung** on the lines.
Then sound out the words you wrote.

1. h u ng
2. l ung
3. sw ung
4. fl ung
5. s ung
6. st ung

Story Words to Know

Say each word in the box. Write a word to complete each sentence.
Then read the sentences.

1. I like to go to **school**.
2. It is so **quiet** at night.
3. I go home **after** school.

after
quiet
school

© Evan-Moor Corp. • EMC 3354 • Word Family Stories and Activities   81

Page 82

Teacher: Read the story to your students.
Name_____

Word Family
-ung

Listen as the story is read to you.
Underline the words in the **-ung** family.
Then read the story to yourself.

After School

It is quiet after school.
The last bell has rung.
The last swing has swung.
The last ball has been flung.
The last song has been sung.
Every coat is hung.
It is so quiet after school!

Take the story home. Read the story to your family.

82   Word Family Stories and Activities • EMC 3354 • © Evan-Moor Corp.

Page 83

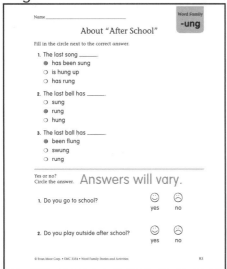

Name_____

Word Family -ung

About "After School"

Fill in the circle next to the correct answer.

1. The last song _____.
   ● has been sung
   ○ is hung up
   ○ has rung

2. The last bell has _____.
   ○ sung
   ● rung
   ○ hung

3. The last ball has _____.
   ● been flung
   ○ swung
   ○ rung

Yes or no?
Circle the answer. **Answers will vary.**

1. Do you go to school? ☺ ☹
   yes no

2. Do you play outside after school? ☺ ☹
   yes no

Page 84

Name_____

Word Family -ung

Write **-ung** Words

Complete the sentences.
Use the words.

clung hung stung swung

1. I _hung_ up my coat.
2. A bee _clung_ to my coat.
3. I _swung_ at the bee.
4. The bee _stung_ me!

Find the word that matches the picture.
Circle it.

1. stung (lung)
2. (flung) hung
3. swung (sung)

Page 87

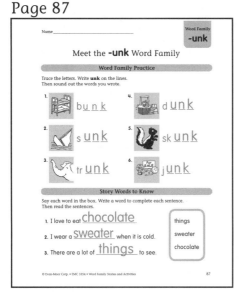

Name_____

Word Family -unk

Meet the **-unk** Word Family

Word Family Practice

Trace the letters. Write **unk** on the lines.
Then sound out the words you wrote.

1. b u n k
2. s unk
3. tr unk
4. d unk
5. sk unk
6. j unk

Story Words to Know

Say each word in the box. Write a word to complete each sentence.
Then read the sentences.

1. I love to eat _chocolate_
2. I wear a _sweater_ when it is cold.
3. There are a lot of _things_ to see.

things
sweater
chocolate

Page 88

Teacher: Read the story to your students.

Name_____

Word Family -unk

Listen as the story is read to you.
Underline the words in the **-unk** family.
Then read the story to yourself.

The Junk Sale

Dad and I went to a junk sale.

We saw a lot of things...
a pretty trunk,
a toy skunk,
a sweater that shrunk,
a bed to bunk,
a boat that sunk,
and a chocolate chunk.

It sure is fun to look at junk!

Take the story home. Read the story to your family.

Page 89

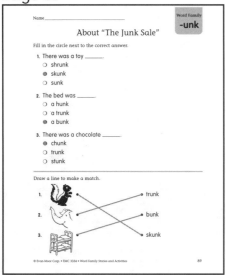

Name_____

Word Family -unk

About "The Junk Sale"

Fill in the circle next to the correct answer.

1. There was a toy _____.
   ○ shrunk
   ● skunk
   ○ sunk

2. The bed was _____.
   ○ a hunk
   ○ a trunk
   ● a bunk

3. There was a chocolate _____.
   ● chunk
   ○ trunk
   ○ stunk

Draw a line to make a match.

1. trunk
2. bunk
3. skunk

Page 90

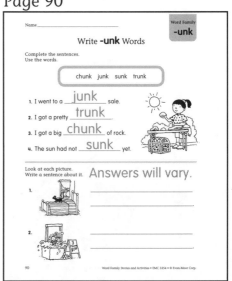

Name_____

Word Family -unk

Write **-unk** Words

Complete the sentences.
Use the words.

chunk junk sunk trunk

1. I went to a _junk_ sale.
2. I got a pretty _trunk_
3. I got a big _chunk_ of rock.
4. The sun had not _sunk_ yet.

Look at each picture.
Write a sentence about it. **Answers will vary.**

1. _____

2. _____

Page 93

Page 94

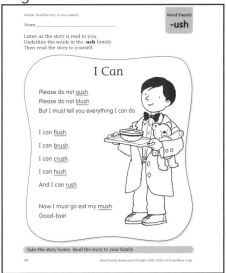

Page 95

Page 96

Bulletin Board

Use the train template to make a word family train for your bulletin board.

Write the word family on the engine of the train and word family words on the boxcars. Reproduce as many boxcars as needed to complete the word family your class has mastered.

Word Family Stories and Activities • EMC 3354 • © Evan-Moor Corp.